What Counts

Based on Ben Franklin's **13 Virtues**

by

Michael L. Loren, M.D.

Overland Park Press
Independence, Missouri

Published by Overland Park Press
17500 Medical Center Parkway, Independence, MO 64057

ISBN : 09641930-0-0
Library of Congress Catalogue Number: 94-67811

Publication design: Allen Simon Productions

10 9 8 7 6 5 4 3 2

Acknowledgments

I wanted to acknowledge Beryl Wein who educated me about the influence of Ben Franklin's Autobiography on European history and how ironic it was that Franklin's ideas never made it into the American home and classroom. My wife, Ann, as a school teacher, continually challenged me with the task of developing a method that could be used by individuals, parents, and teachers. Ed Christophersen suggested it is not enough to have good ideas, but how can the ideas be implemented in a practical way. This manuscript would have never been completed without the encouragement and suggestions of my brother, Cary Loren. My sister, Jackie Lisiecki, made a number of important suggestions that strengthed the manuscript.

I want to thank Martin Rosenberg and Sybil Kaplan for their thoughtful suggestions in editing and improving the manuscript. Allen Simon did an incredible cover and layout. Finally, my parents, Sidney and Lillian Loren, always gave me encouragement and guidance.

To my wife Ann,
and my children Rachel, Daniel, Rebecca and Samuel.
With my love and affection.

Akiva's greatest teacher – drops of water penetrating a rock.

Table of Contents

Introduction

When Ben Franklin was in his twenties, he was quite an idealist. He had developed a system of self-improvement based on examining and improving the virtues in a person. According to Franklin, the virtues that he selected were universal. He made a point to develop a system that did not have any religious bias. His intent was to have a system that would be palatable for any person.

Every morning, for just a few moments, he would focus on one virtue. Often he worked on one virtue each week. He listed thirteen virtues and would restudy them every few months. In the evening, he would reflect on the past day and keep a diary of his progress.

Ben Franklin's system was based on daily self-examination and in essence was a method of continual improvement. I was stunned to realize that this system had never become popular. In the last years of his life, Ben Franklin wrote that he was just too busy with business dealings to do anything about his system. In essence, it was unfinished work.

Currently, American business is recognizing the importance of continual improvement. This concept of total quality management has accounted for the current turnaround of many failing American businesses. However, for a system to be successful, changes and improvement have to be done in small steps. Likewise, in this system of *What Counts*, the focus is on continual individual improvement. This focus of trying to improve ourselves is based on the premise that all of us are not perfect, and we can try to make small changes to make ourselves better individuals.

Some people are not interested in change. They are happy where they are. As long as there is food in their stomachs they are happy. Questions that I raise are: What counts? What is really important? What values are important? How do I conduct myself each day? Do I eat to live or do I live to eat? Do I live so I can see how many pistachio nuts I can stuff in my mouth? Is there more to life than just eating pistachio nuts?

I think that Franklin's system of virtues can serve as a framework for how we can successfully conduct ourselves each day.

MLL

What Counts

Benjamin Franklin was a publisher, printer, author, businessman, scientist, politician, and diplomat. He is noted for Poor Richard's Almanac, scientific studies, and drafting, and the signing of the Declaration of Independence and the United States Constitution. His autobiography (1771) was written to inspire and teach others and is still considered an important work.

His autobiography offers a system of self-improvement, for Franklin recognized his own shortcomings. By actively trying to work on a particular problem, however, he was able to improve himself. Franklin was devoted to the ideal of social progress. Like Franklin, to make change for the better, we need to work on ourselves and improve. We need to do good works. A society is only as good as the individual is good.

Franklin developed the Art of Virtue as a teaching tool. His view was that the Art of Virtue could be taught to children like teaching piano or science. The intent was that the individual would incorporate these teachings in his/her daily living and be a better individual. Franklin believed that the virtues he described were universal and were applicable to all men in all generations. If the individual can improve, then society would be the beneficiary.

Franklin developed a specific system of working on the virtues. He kept a "little book" or diary that listed them, and he mainly focused on one quality each week. Franklin wrote, "I was supriz'd to find myself so much full of faults than I had imagined. But I had the satisfaction of seeing them diminish."

Franklin's intention was that people not just study these thirteen qualities but rather incorporate them in their actions. The end result was good actions.

Franklin was noted for his short, wise comments collected in Poor Richard. "Search others for their virtues, thyself for thy vices," he wrote. When we look at another person it is often easy to be critical and see his or her problems and weaknesses. It is not intended for us to be critical of the weaknesses and failings of others. Part of being a complete person is to try to find the good in others. Often we might want to change a friend or a spouse. One should not bother. It is a waste of time. The only person we have any chance in changing is ourselves.

We often view education as a cure for most of our ills. Scientific and medical advancements are only one part of the equation of an education. We all need to recall with pain how low advanced civilizations can fall. Nazi Germany was a center of culture and scientific advancement while millions burned. Martin Luther King, Jr. said, "We must remember that education is not enough. Intelligence plus character – that is the goal of true education."

I am concerned that we are not meeting our educational goals. Schools are being overloaded with increasingly misbehaving and disrespectful children. I am especially concerned about the increasing use of illegal drugs and violence in our cities and schools. Many children are often left to their own devices and they develop their own system of values. The teachers of children are television and peers. Television and often uneducated peers have taken over the roles traditionally managed by parents.

Franklin recognized that an individual needs to take responsibility for his actions. A person always has the opportunity for self-improvement and change. Even if a person is handicapped by a poor family situation, there is still an opportunity for improvement.

The intention of this essay is to introduce you to Franklin's Virtues. If we all use them daily and try to incorporate them into our lives, hopefully, we will all be wiser, kinder, and more successful in our studies, family, and work.

How do I get started?

Ideally, this writing needs to be reviewed every day – if only for a few moments. Set aside a few minutes each morning in your home. In a classroom setting more time may be needed for group discussions about actual situations or current events that may apply to a particular quality. Frequently the daily newspaper will have examples that facilitate the discussion. The idea of repetition and daily study is especially helpful in young children so they can make it part of their nature. All virtues can be taught to children as young as 5 or 6 years old. This idea of constant self-improvement and repetition is a major part of What Counts. Constant self-improvement has been shown to be important in business. It is also important in ourselves. Of course many of the quotations may have to be modified so they will be understandable for the younger age student.

Everyone asks the question, "How am I going to find time for one more thing to do?" Everybody is busy. We all are being faxed to death. Even spending a few moments once a week is a legitimate way to start. Look at the quotations during breakfast. What if you don't eat breakfast? Everyone needs breakfast. Start eating that raisin bran today!

Each virtue is elaborated on by a quotation which can serve as a focus for a particular day. A quote a day might be a good way to begin. In addition there are suggestions on how to implement a particular virtue followed by additional selected quotations.

All 13 Virtues can be reviewed on a frequent basis. The end result of study is converting them from an idea into an action because good intentions need to be turned into good actions. It is not enough just to learn about them once and then never study them again. It is amazing how short our memories can be. If there is going to be significant individual change and improvement, practice and more practice has to take place. Possibly, over time, some of the 13 Virtues can be integrated into a person's actions while at school, work, or home.

Franklin focused on one main Virtue each week. He kept a journal and tried to measure how he was progressing. Every day his journal served as a constant reminder to him that he had a lot of improving to do.

Each of the 13 Virtues has infinite ways of being viewed. They are like the facets of a diamond. I have selected specific quotations to serve as a focal point. For each Virtue there are numerous quotations to choose which can give you a somewhat different perspective. Many of the Virtues seem to overlap. Qualities of one Virtue may be found in another Virtue. Some quotations may be used in more than one Virtue. All the Virtues share the same underlying theme: be a responsible caring person.

One more final thought. As adults we have a responsibility to serve as examples and to pass on knowledge to the generations following us. Our children and grand-children can learn from us. They learn more from our actions than from our words. If we make a mistake and admit our error, it is a powerful lesson. Although Franklin's intention was for the individual to work on the 13 virtues, this is also a system that can be passed on from parent to child. This is a way to bridge generation gaps. Each virtue has a central core of showing concern and kindness for other people and ourselves. This is probably the essence of what Franklin was trying to accomplish during his life.

Chapter 1

ALERTNESS

Alertness was the first virtue listed by Franklin. His intention was that a person should keep a "coolness and clearness of head." With alertness a person would have more success in pursuing all the other qualities that are listed. With alertness a person could also be educated. In his early years Franklin was concerned about educating himself. He wrote about his intoxicated co-workers and he resolved not to waste his time or money on drinking, but rather to make something of himself.

Alertness also consists of viewing the world fully with thought, enthusiasm and imagination. It requires flexibility and preparedness. It causes us to anticipate problems, to plan ahead until we "see it done". Clarity brings action and will elevate us above the apparent confusion. The idea of "seeing it done" is a great way to reach a goal. The image of a successful bat swing almost guarantees that the real swing will make contact and will be a successful hit.

Danger is often all around us. It is important not to fall into traps. We need to maintain our alertness so we don't get into trouble. Staying alert and keeping a cool head will usually keep us out of trouble.

> You can't depend on your judgment
> when your imagination is out of focus.
>
> *Mark Twain*

Don't be so sure of yourself. Even the best plans may be dead wrong. It is especially bad making decisions when the facts are distorted. We often make assumptions with incomplete information and then act on nonsense information. With education and access to information, our judgment can be improved. Focus often requires insights and concentration. Bring your mind into focus by finding a teacher to study with. Of course not all teachers are so great and it may take a great deal of work to find a teacher to work with. I know I am still looking for a teacher who can tolerate my bad jokes!

> The educated differ from the uneducated
> as much as the living from the dead.
>
> *Aristotle*

It is not always obvious who is educated or uneducated. Today, knowledge is constantly changing. Many of us are being choked to death by publications and journals. The "Information superhighway" is littered with garbage. The differences between the living and the dead are so great. An education gives a person a major advantage over those persons without education. Selective knowledge and careful combing of information are important tools for becoming educated.

> # I have a dream
> that one day this nation will rise up
> and live out the true meaning of its creed:
> "We hold these truths to be self-evident;
> that all men are created equal."
>
> *Martin Luther King, Jr.*

"I have a dream" refers to clarity of thought with a look into the future. Sometimes we have to be careful. Some dreams are created from nonsense and may be misleading. Dreams may need some refinement. "That one day" tells us that now it is not occurring, however, one day it may occur. Maybe that day will be tomorrow. A creed refers to a belief. Although I might have a particular belief, my actions may not transmit my belief to others. Possibly this is a nation in a sleep or a nation ignoring certain truths. Do we also need to have a dream that serves to guide us? King talks about "I" and "this nation." "I" refers to a single person. "Nation" refers to many people. A nation is made up of each one of us. Each one of us needs to have a dream so that this nation will rise up and live.

> Better an empty purse than an empty head.
>
> *German Proverb*

     "An empty purse" refers to not having any money. This is usually a temporary thing and with work a person can earn a living. "An empty head" is often permanent and difficult to change. This might refer to ignorance. Provided a person is willing to open his mind and listen and learn, he may be able to overcome his ignorance. An empty head may possibly be filled. The question is, what do we want to fill our head? Is MTV a good head filler? If a head is filled with nonsense or misinformation, it can be worse than empty. "Better an empty purse" might refer to a person who doesn't have enough. Perhaps he is emptying his purse to pursue fun and pleasure. Filling his head with wisdom may be more lasting and in the long run be more beneficial. It is important that we keep an open mind when we fill our heads with knowledge. We also need to be critical and not too open minded or our brains may fall out.

> Men are not prisoners of fate,
> but only prisoners of their own minds.
>
> *Franklin D. Roosevelt*

"Prisoners of fate" implies a poor situation. How often do we complain and scream about what is happening to us instead of realizing that we can often help control what is occurring? Fate seems so unavoidable. But it does not have to be so! We need to escape from negative thoughts. With wisdom we can escape from this prison of the mind.

Alertness

Alertness - what to do:

1. Go to the library. This is a major, underrated community resource. Librarians can be a great help in pointing you to good writers and periodicals. From books we can get a great education. Classic proven works might be a good starting resource. I would suggest reading Franklin's Autobiography. The main point of being alert is to become educated. Beginning in his childhood, Ben Franklin loved to read books. He would spend any money he saved on books. Franklin had a "thirst for knowledge" and a "bookish inclination." He would set aside time at night and in the early morning for reading. When he became older and prosperous, he started the first free public library system in Philadelphia.

2. Find a teacher with whom to study. In the business community many people learn and advance under the wings of a mentor. There is a resource of older retired teachers, professionals and business people who have had many years of life experience and might be invaluable. Attend free community lectures and conferences. The local chamber of commerce can also be an excellent resource.

3. Interview your potential teacher. Ask about his/her successes and failures. Is this someone with whom you would feel comfortable sharing your own private questions? Is he/she interested in seeing you succeed?

4. Reexamine how you are spending your time. We often get so tied up in events and television shows and doing things, we don't leave room for doing the things that really are important. We often don't have any time to think about what we really want to be doing. Turn off the television and telephone for one evening each week and think about how you really want to spend your time. Then start doing it.

5. Don't depend on alcohol and drugs for relaxation. Alcohol and drugs tend to dull the mind and interfere with any sense of alertness. There are other natural ways to relax without the potentially dangerous adverse medical and mental effects associated with alcohol and drugs.Walking, jogging, yoga, afternoon naps, hobbies and meditation are healthy ways to achieve relaxation.

Alertness

Additional quotations on Alertness:

Nothing in the world is more dangerous than sincere ignorance
        and conscientious stupidity.
        Martin Luther King, Jr.

What is required is sight and insight...
        Then you might add one more: excite.
        Robert Frost

If you keep your mind sufficiently open,
        people will throw a lot of rubbish into it.
        William Orton

It ain't what a man don't know that makes him a fool,
        but what he does know that ain't so.
        Josh Billings

The instruction we find in books is like fire. We fetch it from
       our neighbors, kindle it at home, communicate it to others,
       and it becomes the property of all.

Voltaire

Pain makes man think. Thought makes man wise.
       Wisdom makes life endurable.

John Patrick

The mere imparting of information is not education. Above all things,
       the effort must result in making a man think and do for himself.

Carter G. Woodson

Knowledge is like a garden: if it is not cultivated it cannot be harvested.

Guinea Proverb

Armed with the knowledge of our past,
we can with confidence charter a course for our future.

Malcolm X

Being illiterate is like having handcuffs on all the time.

William Robinson

The doors of the world are open to people who can read.

Sonya Carson

Give a man a fish and you feed him for a day.

Teach a man to fish

and you feed him for a lifetime.

Chinese proverb

Alertness

Notes

Chapter 2

SILENCE

Franklin listed the virtue of silence because "Silence would be more easy, and my desire being to gain knowledge, knowledge...was obtained rather by the use of the ears than of the tongue." Franklin described himself as having a habit of "prattling, punning, and joking." We need to economize our words in speech and writing. "Say little, do much." Listen to our advisors – our parents and teachers.

Silence can also be misused. Clearly there are times when a person needs to speak. Our words can defend a person or situation. Our words can rescue a person who is in distress. If we don't speak up, often our silence is interpreted as agreeing with what was said.

The popular childhood expression "sticks and stones may break my bones but names will never hurt me" is untrue. Many of us have walked through life with permanent wounds which were based on hurtful words given to us by family and friends. When someone hits me, it hurts. The hurt will heal over time. But a well chosen word can attack my very essence and hurt me for the rest of my life.

When talking about others, we often use the expression, "But it is true!" Even when truth is spoken, it can still destroy or harm an individual. According to Franklin:

"Speak not but what may benefit others." Words need to be used with some thought and tact. We have a responsibility to use our words in a nice way. Gossip, sarcasm, and cutdowns may appear to be innocent. Often a cutdown is intended to embarrass a person and it can go to the heart of a person. A cutdown actually is used to make a person look smaller. If he looks smaller, it temporarily makes me look bigger. This is not a nice way to act.

> It is easy to utter what has been kept silent,
> but impossible to recall what has been uttered.
> *Plutarch*

Nasty hurtful thoughts can be turned into words easily. We have a responsibility to be careful with our speech. Once a word is spoken, it cannot be taken back.

There is an old story of a man who embarrassed his best friend with words of gossip spoken to other people. Later he attempted to apologize to the friend. He was told that he could repair what he did by emptying a pillow full of feathers in the wind and then collecting every feather. It was probably an easier task collecting the feathers than recalling what had been said.

> ## Talk does not cook rice.
> *Japanese Proverb*

This is another way of saying, speak little and do much, or actions speak louder than words. At times talk may be needed to educate someone how to cook rice. Our words may precede action, however, there are important things that need to be done. Sometimes talk is overdone and action is needed now. Cook rice is an image of a basic necessity. We all need to eat for survival. It is a poor commentary that in the United States, a nation of such great wealth, there is so much surrounding poverty in our cities and countryside. There is much work to be done.

Sticks and stones are hard on bones.
Aimed with angry art,
Words can sting like anything.
But silence breaks the heart.

Phylis McGinley

The injury of being hurt in a fight is temporary and most of us will recover. The carefully chosen word can destroy a person and may have a lasting effect years after they are spoken. Silence can be used in a positive way to learn and improve communication, however, many times it can have devastating effects. Listen to the silence while an elderly person dies of loneliness. Listen to the pain of silence when brothers refuse to talk for years because of a trivial misunderstanding. Listen to the screams of silence as we watch millions die of starvation or refugees turned away from freedom.

Silence - what to do:

1. **When talking to another person, give him/her time to say what he/she has to say.** Sometimes if I don't respond immediately, but pause in my speech, the other person may say more and reveal what is really important.

2. **Speak little and do much.** Don't make too many promises. Surprise the other person by doing more than is expected. I once saw this sign at a car rental place: *Don't promise the customer more than you can deliver and deliver more than you promise.*

3. **Speak up when you see an apparent injustice occur**. Often it is easy not getting involved. After all, we are all busy and who has the time to help out someone who may be in trouble? If we don't get involved, we are silently agreeing with the injustice. Speak up by first examining the situation. If I weigh the evidence and believe that a wrong has occurred, I will often write letters to newspapers, congressmen, and senators asking for some support.

4. **Be sensitive to words being used in a conversation**. Gossiping about other people is a difficult habit to break. Hearing a baby scream makes many of us want to leave the room; likewise we need to equate gossip with a baby's scream.

5. **If a discussion of a person occurs, and the words are spoken negatively about the person or in a hurtful way, divert the conversation immediately**. Most of us talk in a disjointed way, skipping from topic to topic. The phrase, "By the way, that reminds me of ... " followed by diverting information such as statistics from The Guinness Book of Records is quite helpful. Directly saying "I don't talk about other people behind their backs" is often effective.

6. **Don't talk about other people behind their backs unless the conversation can be used in a way to help the person**. "I am sorry that Jan is getting a divorce, I think that this will be a rough time for her. Is there anything I can do to help?"

7. **The truth can be painful at times**. Sometimes it is better not speaking. Revealing the truth may sometimes hurt someone and may not serve any useful purpose. In such a situation it is better to keep quiet. When seeing a misbehaving child in a store, to tell the mother to improve her discipline skills will only aggravate her.

8. **When I am angry and I correct my child**, I find it better, at times, not to speak at that moment but to delay what I have to say until I have a clearer head later that day.

Ben Franklin noticed that he had a tendency to socialize and joke. He was intent on breaking this habit. I doubt that he was able to stop the jokes, because he was a very funny guy. In addition, he recognized that he was often dogmatic in his conversations and all too often his words got him into trouble. He quickly realized he was more effective by being careful about not contradicting others. He realized with listening he also had an opportunity to learn.

Silence

Additional Quotes on Silence:

Better slip with foot than with tongue.

Ben Franklin

The right word may be effective,
but no word was ever as effective as a rightly timed pause.

Mark Twain

I have often regretted my speech, never my silence.

Publilius Syrus

The tongue is more to be feared than the sword.

Japanese proverb

Too much talk will include errors.

Burmese Proverb

It is better to keep your mouth shut and appear stupid
than to open it and remove all doubt.

Mark Twain

Even doubtful accusations leave a stain behind them.

Thomas Fuller, M.D.

Give every man thine ear, but few thy voice.

Shakespeare

Silence is not always golden and it is tact that is golden, not silence.

Samuel Butler

A silent tongue does not betray its owner.

African Proverb

The silence between your words/ rams into me/ like a sword.

Alice Walker

To speak without thinking
is to shoot without aiming.

Spanish proverb

Notes

Chapter 3

ORDER

According to Franklin, order was his most difficult virtue to follow. Franklin was brilliant, however he often had multiple pans cooking in a fire at one time and at times it was hard for him to decide which task should be worked on and completed. Franklin said, "Let all your things have their places. Let each part of your business have its time." It is much easier doing one task at a time. Often when we attempt to work on two or three projects simultaneously we accomplish nothing. Sometimes we end up ruining the meal.

How often do we waste time looking for things that are misplaced? Clutter can sometimes serve as a trigger generating new ideas. However it can also lead to inefficiency and loss of direction. When studying, one should do it at the same time and place each day. With order an apparently overwhelming project can be a possibility. Work one step at a time.

Are there extremes of being too orderly or having a lack of order? Certainly! Often I get so wrapped up in the method of doing something, the task may not get completed.

> ## Order is the shape upon which beauty depends.
> *Pearl S. Buck*

Order is a framework on which our actions depend. With order we have some method so we can be more focused. "Upon which beauty depends" – possibly beauty refers to creativity and discovery. This can refer to the arts and sciences. Discovery needs order. Which order? There are infinite methods of order. Even in my small room, if I make order from chaos, I can create beauty. The beauty I create may relax me and give me peace.

> "Begin at the beginning," the king said, gravely, "and go till you come to the end; then stop."
>
> *Lewis Carroll*

"Begin at the beginning"... Where else should one begin? To begin a task, it has to be started in an orderly fashion. Often critical steps are overlooked and will result in failure. "Gravely" refers to taking the task seriously with slow steps. If it is an important task, begin slowly and plan your attack. Every project has an ending. Do not drag it out endlessly. Complete it, then get on to a new project.

> Ill habits gather by unseen degrees,
> As brooks make rivers, rivers run to seas. *Ovid*

Bad habits often creep up upon us without our being aware. "Habits gather" refers to habits that may not have been a part of our life, then they enter. From whom do we gather these habits? We gather habits from our friends and associations. Small, bad habits lead to larger bad habits. There is an order to the development of "ill habits." What are bad habits? How can we avoid them? Is there an order or method of developing good habits at work and at home? According to my mother, I only have good habits. My wife can always point out my bad habits.

> There is a best way of doing everything.
> If it be to boil an egg. *Emerson*

Every action that we take can have multiple ways of being completed. But how do we know if what has always been done is really the best way? Maybe we can develop a new way of doing something, even if it is to boil an egg. Even a task as simple as boiling an egg has a correct method.

Order - what to do:

1. **Get a day planner**. This is a helpful tool. I use it to list the things I need to do for the day. Items that are not done for the day can easily be moved ahead to the next day or another day during the month. Items to do can be prioritized in order or importance. I use a system of A= very important; this is a critical thing, like going for a walk, going out for dinner with my wife, or attending a child's basketball game. B= necessary to do, but not critical such as paying the rent, doing a task for the office. C= minor hassles that can be passed up and done any day like cutting the grass or painting the house.

2. **Make a separate list of what you intend to accomplish.** A list of long-term goals and short-term goals can be helpful. Long-term goals are things that I may want to be doing at home or work that I would like to be doing but which I haven't accomplished yet. These lists are my long term plans. An example of long term goals might be a change of occupation, or involvement in a social organization such as the Boy Scouts. Examples of short term goals might be planning a canoe trip with family, or learning a foreign language.

3. There is an order to things and if a difficult problem is broken into small parts and tackled one step at a time, in a short time the problem will be completed. One of the secrets of completion is to outline the steps needed to reach that goal. Franklin was a chess addict. Chess is a game based on strategy and order. To play well requires looking ahead, planning, and stringing together 'what if' scenarios. Chess is a good game to learn for practicing order and strategy.

4. Don't let your "to do" list sit. Procrastination is a difficult habit to break. Often distasteful actions are hard to start, however, if they are first put on a list, it is a beginning step. The first step still needs to be done. I find myself listing distasteful actions as high priority, however, I pass them off quickly and focus on the trivial stuff for the day. Sometimes, in order to do a difficult task, I find myself putting aside the minor stuff.

5. Ben Franklin kept a "little book" which listed his virtues and what he would do each day. In a sense he developed his own day planner. He felt that this book kept his goals in front of him. He could focus on improving his habits and also keep better track of his daily affairs. By planning out each day he felt he could accomplish more. Early in the morning he would contemplate what his affairs would be for the day. For the last five years I have been using a day planner which I take everywhere. Recently I had it waterproofed so I could use it in the shower.

Additional quotations on Order:

Plans get you into things, but you got to work your way out.

Will Rogers

The mightiest rivers lose their force when split up into several streams.

Ovid

Out of intense complexities intense simplicities emerge.

Winston Churchill

Without oars, you cannot cross in a boat.

Japanese Proverb

Order marches with weighty and measured strides; disorder is always
in a hurry. ...We often get in quicker by the back door than by the front.

Napoleon I

Do not plan for ventures before finishing what's at hand.

Euripides

If there are obstacles, the shortest line between two points
may be the crooked line.

Bertolt Brecht

Amid a multitude of projects, no plan is devised....
It is a bad plan that admits no modification.   *Publilius Syrus*

There is time enough for everything in the course of a day
  if you do but one thing at once;
but there is not time enough in the year
  if you will do two things at a time.

        Lord Chesterfield

One arrow does not bring down two birds.

        Turkish proverb

Education is our passport to the future,
for tomorrow belongs to the people who prepare for it today.

        Malcolm X

To make preparation does not spoil the trip.

        Guinea Proverb

Notes

Notes

Order

Notes

Chapter 4
RESOLUTION

Franklin said, "Resolve to perform what you ought. Perform without fail what you resolve." Stick to your plan. Focus your limited energies and complete your actions. Many of us make promises or have wishes. Things will not happen unless we act. Prior to action, careful thought is needed. Careful thought will often lead to proper actions. Consult with people who can serve as advisors such as parents, grandparents, friends, and teachers.

Sometimes a course of action is not clear. Information may be spotty or contradictory. We may need to hesitate. Meet again with advisors. There are times when we may have to act and there are still doubts. Our choice may be well thought out, but nevertheless an error occurs. This happens to many of the best laid out plans. "Pick yourself up again." Refocus on your plan, problem, or goal.

Valuable discoveries and worthwhile projects do not come easy. Failure is common. In science, most laboratory experiments fail. An important lesson is learning from a mistake.

A good advisor can save us from the wasted time of repeating the same mistakes which others have done in the past.

Athletes in all sports usually do not start out successful. They all need to practice. To be good at something takes lots of work. Be resolved. With a goal in our head, we will succeed. Our mental attitude often makes the difference between success and failure.

> ## You may be disappointed if you fail,
> ## but you are doomed if you don't try.
> *Beverly Sills*

If I fail, I may possibly be disappointed. A disappointment does not have to be a permanent failing just because things did not work out. There is always the opportunity to try again. If I never try, how can I possibly succeed? Success may not come easily, but it requires action and practice. Take a chance and act.

> Parents can only give good advice or put them
> on the right paths, but the final forming of a person's
> character lies in their own hands.
>
> *Anne Frank*

Our parents may influence us when we are young children. Still we may deviate from what they intended. And what if my parents don't care about me? What if they give me bad advice? What if I am on the wrong path for me? Then I will be on a more difficult path. Actually, I may end up falling on my face more easily. Possibly I can find the right path. It is not an easy task. We all have weak qualities which could stand for some improvement. Don't blame unfortunate circumstance on parents. Accept that the future is really in our hands. We can do a great deal, provided we resolve to make it a priority.

Resolution

> If you wish to learn the highest truth,
> you must begin with the alphabet.
> *Japanese proverb*

The desire to learn has to come from inside. We need to be motivated. Sometimes we can find a teacher to help motivate us to get on the right path. The "highest truth" refers to what really counts. The alphabet is the most basic thing that we all learn. To get to high truths requires simplicity in thought and action. It is common to get distracted and tied up with events that are good for the moment but don't have much intrinsic value.

> Habit is habit,
> and not to be flung out of the window by any man,
> but coaxed downstairs a step at a time.
> *Mark Twain*

It is a slow process to change habits and to take on new habits. What we may want to change needs to be done slowly or it will not stick. Stay on track and slowly things will improve, but it must be one step at a time. It takes a great deal of courage to follow a path of improvement. There may be many discouragements. There may be times when we will fall quickly down. But just as quickly as we may fall off track, like a rubber band, we have the ability to snap back to a higher level.

Resolution – what to do:

1. **When working with the To Do list, first work on the high priority items**. Break the project into small steps and do one step at a time.

2. **To imagine successful completion can also be helpful**. Find a quiet place for a few minutes, either early in the morning or late at night. Relax. Relax your muscles, turn your arms and legs into spaghetti. Close your eyes, take a few deep breaths and imagine doing the project and completing it. Imagine all the steps to reach completion. Often the imaging will lead you to action and completion.

3. **Stress, conflicts, and problems at home, school or work will interfere with our ability to reach success**. These distractions will interfere with our ability to act. A difficult skill is being able to tune out the distractions and difficult situations so that we can successfully get going and begin what is really important. Many individuals used humor and denial strategies to focus away from distractions. Bothersome thoughts can sometimes be managed with relaxation training, deep breathing and physical activity.

Resolution

4. Resolve to do what you must do. Difficult challenges may seem insurmountable. Many of us would more readily try something new if we had more encouragement from family and friends. Many times our closest friends and relatives try to discourage us. Discussing the challenge with someone who has successfully done what we are planning to do is very helpful.

Ben Franklin was very creative. He had dozens of ideas and plans going through his brain every day. After a project was thought, he arranged all the items necessary to make it a success, and then he put his energy into the project until it came to completion. He was not easily discouraged. There were many problems which he had to face. He was bull headed in his desire to succeed, and he would not allow hunger or lack of money get into the way of his goal of success.

Additional quotations on Resolution:

It is still one of the tragedies of human history that the 'children of darkness'
are frequently more determined and zealous than the 'children of light.'

Martin Luther King, Jr.

What people say you cannot do, you try and find that you can.

Henry David Thoreau

Do not be afraid of the past.
If people tell you that it is irrevocable, do not believe them.

Oscar Wilde

Between two stools we sit on the ground.

French Proverb

One of these days is none of these days.

English Proverb

What may be done at any time will be done at no time.

Thomas Fuller

Delay is preferable to error.

Thomas Jefferson

Success is the result of perfection, hardwork, learning from failure, loyalty and persistence.

Colin Powell

Many persons have a wrong idea of what constitutes true happiness. It is no attained through self-gratification, but through fidelity to a worthy purpose.

Helen Keller

Some minds seem almost to create themselves, springing up under every disadvantage and working their solitary but irresistible way through a thousand obstacles.

Washington Irving

If you run, you might lose.
If you don't run,
you're guaranteed to lose.

Jesse L. Jackson

Notes

Chapter 5
CONSERVATION

Franklin said, "Make no expense but to do good to others or yourself." Waste nothing. Use time wisely. There are not enough resources. We do not have enough time and money for all people and all programs, so first take care of the needs of ourselves and our family then go beyond to our closer friends and our community.

I find myself eaten alive by lack of time. Often I am over committed to too many people, committees, and activities. More than 24 hours in a day are needed to complete what has to be done. I find it helpful to make a list of the really important things that need completion. My time needs to be conserved. It is so easy getting caught in a swamp of nonsense and trivia. We all need one day each week when we turn off the phones and television and recharge our batteries. It can be a day spent recognizing the beauty in our friends, family and the world around us.

Conservation has traditionally focused on saving land, water, resources, and energy. We can also focus on using people maximally instead of wasting them. Not having enough time is a major problem which we all face. The main focus of conservation needs to be using our time, money and resources in an efficient way to make our lives worthwhile and happy.

> Simplicity, simplicity, simplicity!
> I say, let your affairs be as two or three,
> and not a hundred or a thousand;
> instead of a million count half a dozen,
> and keep your accounts on your thumb-nail.
>
> *Thoreau*

Work at keeping things simple. We are living in a complicated time with busy schedules, cable television, instant news, and information overload. To simplify is an active process of avoiding complications. Cut down on the commitments. Schedule free time. If you imagine your life is over and you are ready for the grave, you will quickly focus on doing only what is necessary. No one will disagree that a good goal in life is to be a happy person. Maybe simplicity is one way to reach that goal.

> **I believe we would be happier to have a personal revolution in our individual lives and go back to simpler living and more direct thinking. It is the simple things in life that make living worthwhile, the sweet fundamental things such as love and duty, work and rest and living close to nature.**
>
> *Laura Ingalls Wilder*

It may require a major change to reach a goal of a happier life. Does happiness refer to the satisfaction of recognizing what really counts? For many of us, simplicity is a new experience. We get caught up in complications. We need to relearn the alphabet. It is the simple things in life which make living worthwhile. "Living worthwhile" means that life has a value, and we need to recognize how high this value is. We have a responsibility to care for the deserted and the lonely, the old and the infirm. The lives of millions of adults and children are being ignored and wasted each day. It seems easier for me to talk about millions of people starving in Africa than for me to talk about a single sick elderly neighbor. True, I cannot take care of everyone, but I can help myself and those around me.

> The biggest disease today is not leprosy or Tuberculosis, but rather the feeling of being unwanted, uncared for and deserted by everyone.
>
> *Mother Teresa*

Mother Teresa is not talking about just any disease. This is a disease on a world class level. Most disease needs to be approached by finding a cure or a way of controlling the illness. "Is not leprosy or Tuberculosis" refers to illnesses which we can point to and control with money and technology. Is this a disease that is not recognized? This is a silent disease! "But rather the feeling of being unwanted, uncared for and deserted by everyone," questions, why do people have these feelings of loneliness? Do I contribute to your loneliness? How do I cure being unwanted, uncared for and deserted? If I only pursue happiness for myself, will I be sensitive to this biggest disease? Is the biggest disease located in my home? If I am only for myself, what am I?

Conservation – what to do:

1. **Devoting our time and money to community service is a simple way of implementing this virtue**. I have seen successful businessmen, lawyers, doctors, and others spend time with their own children and other children in worthwhile programs like big brother and scouts and not only impact on others, but also gain a great deal of personal satisfaction that they were adding to society. There are many service and religious organizations that need volunteers to work in hospitals, hospices and nursing facilities. Volunteers are desperately needed to assist teachers in public schools. Adults are needed to teach the millions of adults in America who are illiterate. Many of these programs will train you.

2. **Decaying inner cities and high unemployment rates are a major strain on our society.** We need creative leaders to develop garden industries and the regreening of the vacant lots.

3. Our time is in short supply. A day planner can be helpful in organizing items, however, it can also have the dark side of allowing us to schedule ourselves with no breathing room. We need moments to escape so we can relax and enjoy our lives. There are some days when I make an effort to schedule nothing. Sometimes we can be slaves to ringing phones and pagers. Who said I have to answer the phone because it is ringing? Some evenings I turn off the ringer on the phone. I also use an answering machine to help retrieve messages.

4. Franklin intended conservation to lead to financial independence. With financial independence a person can contribute more to society rather than be a burden to it. Franklin's intention was for a person to use his financial resources in a prudent fashion. What can a person do? Buy a modest car. Live in a home that will not stretch you with a high monthly payment. Try to avoid buying items with credit cards unless you can pay off the balance each month. When buying clothing, go after classic styles that will not go out of style and get quality so they will last and you won't have to spend as much time shopping.

Additional quotes on Conservation:

Time is the coin of your life. It is the only coin you have,
and only you can determine how it will be spent.
Be careful lest you let other people spend it for you.

Carl Sandburg

Beware of little expenses. A small leak will sink a great ship...
ere you consult your fancy, consult your purse.   *Ben Franklin*

Half our life is spent trying to find something to do with the time
we have rushed through life trying to save.   *Will Rogers*

Saving time, it seems, has a primacy that's too rarely examined.

Ellen Goodman

Less is more.

Robert Browning

The ability to simplify means to eliminate the unnecessary
so that the necessary may speak.

Hans Hofmann

We must use time creatively,
and forever realize that the time
is always ripe to do right.

Nelson Mandela

Notes

Chapter 6

INDUSTRY

"Lose no time," Franklin said. "Be always employed in something useful." Franklin is encouraging us to begin working as soon as possible and to find work that will give us satisfaction that we are accomplishing something. Having satisfaction in work is an inner attitude. It doesn't really matter what type of work a person does. Even if we don't really accomplish much with our work, if we view that what we are doing has a purpose, we will more likely maintain a positive attitude about work. Work can often give us a sense of self-worth and much happiness. Many of us need ongoing encouragement and feedback that we are appreciated and what we are doing is important.

There are so many things that need to be discovered and improved. The day is short, there is much work to be done, and often we don't have the motivation to get going. During the early 1900's, the director of the United States Patent Office approached President McKinley and suggested that the patent office be closed: "We have the telegraph, steamship, and railroad. After all, what more could possibly be invented?"

> The world is sown with good; but unless I turn my
> glad thoughts into practical living and till my own field,
> I cannot reap a kernel of the good.
>
> *Helen Keller*

We often have good intentions and good thoughts toward other people. What good are words without action? Don't tell me how much you love me; show me! Don't till my field, work on your field. Improve your own garden or it will be filled with weeds. "Practical living" refers to day to day mundane activities. Even saying a simple "hello" to a person requires action. Ordinary actions can make a big difference in our life and the life of others. Look how much happiness we can deliver to a person by just smiling "hello."

> ## A man who does not leave his hut will bring nothing in.
> ### *West African proverb*

It is so easy to stay where I am and not try. A hut or home is comfort and familiar. I am content to stay where I am. If I do not go out, how will I improve my situation? If I do not try something new, how will I advance? If a salesman expects to make a sale, he needs to keep knocking on doors. Don't sit still. To overcome hardship, we need to hustle.

> ## *Diligence is the Mother of Good-Luck.*
> ### *Ben Franklin*

Diligence refers to planning, long hours, and hard work. Good Luck occurs more often with some people because their work habits and plans lead them to a higher percent of wins and success. Some people appear to be making a gamble in business, but because of their knowledge and experience, it really is a sure thing.

> ## Miracles sometimes occur,
> ## but one has to work
> ## terribly hard for them.
> *Chaim Weizmann*

Miracles are events that seem unbelievable and are often actions that we would never believe would occur. What seems impossible becomes possible with much thought and hard work.

> ## Our greatest weariness comes from work not done.
> *Eric Hoffer*

Preoccupation or ideas on what needs to be completed can dominate our thoughts. The assignment or task may get blown out of proportion until it is actually worked on. Consider how much relaxed we are when the work is completed.

Industry

Industry – what to do:

1. **One of the worst problems that occurs with any business is wasting time**. Talking on the phone, visiting with friends, long breaks and basically not maintaining an interest at the work place are poor work habits. Good habits begin at home. My children are basically glued to the couch when it comes to doing the home chores of dishes, yard work, and keeping their room picked up. I am not doing them any good when I don't tell them how I expect things to be in our home. We all need some encouragement and direction to maintain good work habits.

2. **Television watching is a major cause of lost productivity**. It is an addictive habit – coming home and plopping down in front of the set. Once a week I would recommend turning off the television if only for a few hours. Use those few hours to read, go for a walk, visit a park with your child, visit a library or museum, or have a dinner with family and friends.

3. **We can only think so much and then we must act if we intend to accomplish anything**. So how do we start? The simple work of greeting a person might start with the idea of wanting to be friends. Until I actually open my mouth, say hello, and put a sincere smile on my face, I have not accomplished anything.

4. **Work that we do needs to be examined daily**. Can things be improved? Often we get caught in repetitive ways of doing our work and there is a perception that there is no room for improvement. View change as a healthy way to make ourselves more successful. Make small changes. In my office I will often present a small problem to different workers and ask them how they might solve the problem. Input from other people may give me insight on how to proceed. Frustrating problems can be an opportunity for improvement.

5. **Ben Franklin started each day early in the morning**. Usually he was up by five a.m. He spent the early morning washing, meditating and then resolving in his mind what he would be planning for the day. This was a critical time because it set the tone and direction for the rest of the day. He would ask himself each morning: What good shall I do this day? In the evening, just prior to going to sleep he would ask the question: What good have I done today? My question is: what kind of alarm clock did he use? Most of us are using clocks with snooze alarms. Some of those snooze alarms never seem to wake us up.

Additional quotations on Industry:

It's not enough to be busy... the question is: what are we busy about?
Henry David Thoreau

My father taught me to work, but not to love it. I never did like work, and I don't deny it. I'd rather read, tell stories, crack jokes, talk, laugh – anything but work.
Abraham Lincoln

Work spares us from three great evils: boredom, vice, and need.
Voltaire

The day is short, the labor long, the workers are idle, and reward is great, and the Master is urgent.
Tarfon

How do I work? I grope.

Albert Einstein

When you cease to make a contribution, you begin to die.

Eleanor Roosevelt

Never let work drive you, master it and keep in complete control.

Booker T. Washington

Idleness is a mother. She has a son: robbery, and a daughter: hunger.

Victor Hugo

A sleepy man catches no fish

Maltese Proverb

Pride and laziness are the keys of poverty.

Hispanic Proverb

In work there is good fortune.

Arab Proverb

Notes

Chapter 7
SINCERITY

$\mathbb{A}$ ccording to Franklin, one should, "Think innocently and justly; and if you speak, speak accordingly." Sincerity combines truthfulness with concern for the other person. Speaking words with sincerity includes being direct and not misleading. Even before we speak, recognize the feelings of the other person. Sincerity is a reflection of what kind of person I am. If I am sincere, people will trust and confide in me. Avoid tricking or tripping up someone. Avoid misleading people. Don't let words convince you, but rather depend on good actions to define the sincerity of the person.

Can we be truthful and hurt someone? Are there circumstances when the truth is too brutal? How the truth is presented may determine its effect. There are times when it is better to withhold the truth. The truth always needs to be presented with sensitivity and kindness.

> A little sincerity is a dangerous thing, and a great deal of it is absolutely fatal.
> *Oscar Wilde*

Sincerity requires a balance. Sometimes telling the truth can be brutal. It is sometimes better to hold your tongue. Being sincere requires tact. Mix kindness with sincerity, otherwise, being sincere to a fault can be downright nasty.

> **Truth is mighty and will prevail. There is nothing the matter with this, except that it ain't so.**
> *Mark Twain*

In the end truth will usually rise up and show itself over falsehoods. This often takes time and patience. We would like to believe that truth will eventually show up, however, falsehoods have a tendency to dominate and are often hard to eradicate. Often what we have believed to be true is found to be dead wrong. History books throughout the world are full of many revised accounts of what "really happened." Racism, sexism, anti-Semitism have been maintained for generations and they still exist today. The truth is often presented but some people aren't interested in listening.

> I have tried to be honest.
> To be honest is to confront the truth.
> However unpleasant and inconvenient the truth may be,
> I believe we must expose and face it if we are to achieve
> a better quality of American life.
>
> *Martin Luther King, Jr.*

It is common for me to take the easy way and pretend that I am doing the right thing. Often I will find myself making up rationalizations and excuses for my mistakes. I will cover up what I did. I will blame others for my errors. Confronting the truth requires action. Confrontation is usually not pleasant. The truth often hurts. I need to take more responsibility for what I do. The apparent truth is often covered with falsehoods. It is similar to an apple. It may look beautiful on the outside, but when you peel off the skin, the inside may be rotted. Let's examine the apple and see if it is good on the inside. For me to make any progress, I will have to examine what I am and where I am going.

Sincerity – what to do:

1. I recognize that my words can have an effect on those people to whom I speak. Words are not innocent sounds or grunts. With my words I can ruin a friendship or I can make one. Speaking with sincerity means to be thoughtful about the other person's feelings. If I think that my words may hurt the other person, I make sure that what is being said is not for my personal gain, and it can be used constructively by the other person.

2. When I am dealing with an explosive situation, I often ask myself, "How would I like someone to speak to me about this?" Sometimes I get a second opinion and consult with my wife and ask her how to word things. There have been many times when I write down what I will say to make sure that I don't say something I may regret later. I may jot down a few phrases on a note card and review it before I have the meeting.

3. **Sincerity includes speaking with honesty**. I am not implying that we may have to lie at times, however, there are situations when it is better to be quiet and not reveal what we might know. This takes a great deal of individual strength and insight. I usually evaluate the situation in terms of how important is my sharing the information. Will I get pleasure sharing the information? If I am getting a charge out of telling something but it will be at the expense of someone else, then I usually will not share the information.

4. **How do we know that we are really speaking the truth?** Frequently we can be misled by our egos and think that we are in the right but we are definitely mistaken. We need to be careful that what we are saying is not misunderstood and is not misleading. We have a responsibility to modify our position if we later find that we are mistaken. Often times I will say something that was in error and I then have to correct myself.

5. **A direct, in-person apology is more effective than a phone call**. In addition, writing a letter of apology solidifies what we sincerely mean. A sincere letter is more effective than a phone call that may easily be forgotten. The letter gives us the opportunity to be careful in choosing our words and is something the reader can review.

Additional quotations on Sincerity:

Keep away from people who try to belittle your ambitions.
Small people always do that, but the really great
make you feel that you, too, can become great.

Mark Twain

Get the facts first. You can distort them later.

Mark Twain

The truth is rarely pure and never simple.

Oscar Wilde

To be persuasive, we must be believable.
To be believable, we must be credible.
To be credible, we must be truthful.

Edward R. Murrow

A false friend and a shadow attend only while the sun shines.

Ben Franklin

You can fool too many of the people too much of the time.

James Thurber

One who digs a hole for another may fall in himself.

Russian Proverb

Sincerity

You must speak straight
so that your words may go
like sunlight to our hearts.

Cochise of the Apaches

Every truth has two sides.

It is well to look at both,

before we commit ourselves to either.

Aesop

Notes

Chapter 8
JUSTICE

"Wrong none, by doing injuries or omitting the benefits that are your duty," Franklin wrote. Justice is a harsh term. It implies judging and following a correct, perfect unwavering path. In reality, judgments are often based on compromises and misinformation and are usually imprecise. Possibly Franklin was concerned about being fair and minimizing any harm that might occur. I might believe that I am absolutely correct and later find out that I was dead wrong. In my dealings with friends, family and business associates it is best to judge people in a fair way by giving them the benefit of the doubt. Often times I may be missing background information and I may come to a conclusion that may be in error.

If you see a wrong occurring, try to understand more about it. Study it. Gather as much data as you can. Sense the "evil" that may be occurring. Be sensitive to the hurt. Do not be foolish in your actions. Act within the law. If you don't act, you are adding to the injustice.

> Every man must decide whether he will walk
> in the light of creative altruism or the darkness of destruc-
> tive selfishness. This is the judgment.
> Life's most persistent and urgent question is,
> What are you doing for others?
>
> *Martin Luther King, Jr.*

I have free choice to choose how I will act. Will I act justly? Will I choose to extend myself and reach out to another person and be a friend? Will I choose to ignore those around me and instead focus on my own inadequacy or selfish wants? There is so much that needs to be done. Just action is needed not good intentions.

> The possibility that we may fail in the struggle
> ought not to deter us from the support of a cause
> we believe to be just.
>
> *Abraham Lincoln*

There are always losers and winners in any fight. Unfortunately no person can win all the time. The odds of winning may look great and I can still loose. If the odds of winning are against me, I may be reluctant to fight. It takes commitment to back something in which we believe. It is easy to get discouraged. It is easy to be passive and silent when confronting injustice. As Garfield the Cat might say, " Someone else can deal with the injustice; pass me the chips."

> Human kindness has never weakened the stamina
> or softened the fiber of a free people.
> A nation does not have to be cruel to be tough.
> *Franklin D. Roosevelt*

It is not a sign of weakness to show kindness. Kindness refers to actions that help a family member, neighbor, or a stranger. If I help someone, my strength and the direction I follow will not be weakened. Helping someone requires me to give up something. I give up my time, energy and money, however by my giving up something, we all become stronger. In a country without freedom, kindness is actively suppressed. Human kindness will undercut the domination of a dictatorship. We can be firm and kind at the same time. We do not have to be unrelentingly severe.

> # Rigid Injustice is the greatest Injustice. *Thomas Fuller*

"Rigid injustice" implies there is no flexibility or sensitivity. There are times when I need to be more sensitive and less harsh. My harshness may cause more harm than good. Judgment needs to be focused on my actions and not the actions of others. Have I acted fairly? Have I caused harm to the other guy? Am I acting in a just way to my friend? Have I ignored those less fortunate than myself?

> # The highest result of education is tolerance. *Helen Keller*

A goal for each of us is not just learning facts and technology, but rather learning to work with other people. Tolerance might refer to judging others favorably. If I have no patience, I may become intolerant. Am I dogmatic? Can I maintain an open mind and listen to opinions to which I may disagree? Am I so convinced that I am right that I may be blinded to the correct path? Is intolerance at the root of prejudice and hate?

Justice – what to do:

1. We need to be careful that our actions do not cause harm to others. We can harm people in many ways. Sometimes we can be pretty critical of other people. I try to give people the benefit of any doubts and to look at a person and his actions in a favorable light, but this takes a lot of practice. Some people are very obnoxious and it can be hard at times showing sympathy toward them.

2. When an injustice seems to be occurring, I think all of us need to get involved. Simply writing a letter to a congressman may be a first step in correcting an injustice. Involvement in the political and judicial system may be an effective way of correcting a difficult situation.

3. We have a responsibility to correct any errors that we may have made that resulted in harming another person. We need to swallow our pride, admit our error and reimburse the other person for any injury or damages which we may have caused.

4. As adults we need to restrain ourselves from hitting young children. Firm scolding, silent stares, and time out are examples of successful responses than can be used to discipline a child without having to forcibly harm the child. For misbehaving children, startle them with a firm shout statement such as, "Stop hitting!"

5. Some children will use hitting as a rationale for settling disputes. I have heard of young children who view themselves as enforcers of justice in their school. This is an euphemistic way of justifying being a bully and this is inappropriate. Violence does not have to be a natural way of life. Children need to be told in a firm and kind way to keep their hands to themselves and not to hit other children. Hitting is a learned behavior that should not be tolerated.

6. Violence in movies and television seems to be a normal way of life which is having a serious adverse effect on our children. By 15 years of age the average child has witnessed thousands of murders, and countless acts of violence and rapes on television. Human life is not given much of a priority. Taking justice in our hands and beating someone to death seems to be a natural part of our society. We need to oppose media violence through education, organizations and legislation. Set limits on what children view at home and at the movies.

7. Using violence to settle disputes is not right. Many children are carrying guns and other weapons to school for self-defense and offense. The weapons are used to enforce their way and in a sense bring justice to the school ground. This is not appropriate. We need to aggressively oppose these problems and make schools and neighborhoods safe for all of us.

Additional quotations on Justice:

It is no profit to have learned well, if you neglect to do well.

Publilius Syrus

When you are right you cannot be too radical;
    when you are wrong you cannot be too conservative.

Martin Luther King, Jr

There are times when even justice brings harm with it.

Sophocles

Where, after all, do universal human rights begin?
In small places, close to home –
so close and so small that they cannot be seen on any map of the world.
Yet they are the world of the individual person, the neighborhood he lives in,
the school or college he attends, the factory, farm or office where he works.
Such are the places where every man, woman and child seeks equal justice,
equal opportunity, equal dignity without discrimination. Unless these rights
have meaning there, they have little meaning anywhere.

Eleanor Roosevelt

If you stop to be kind, you must swerve often from your path.

Mary Webb

Injustice anywhere is a threat to justice everywhere.

Martin Luther King Jr.

No act of kindness, no matter how small, is ever wasted.

Aesop

Recompense injury with justice, and recompense kindness with kindness.

Confucius

Justice

Notes

Chapter 9
MODERATION

"Avoid Extremes. Forbear resenting injuries so much as you think they deserve," said Franklin. Trying to do things in moderation is not always easy. There is a common expression that we should walk along a straight and narrow path. The challenges that we face each day are not so easy and instead of being straight forward are more like a jagged crevice. If we continue walking in a straight line with our eyes closed, we will more likely crash into a brick wall. Being adaptable to changing situations may make a frustrating day more tolerable.

All the virtues listed by Franklin can be done with moderation. All virtues in extreme can cause error and misunderstanding. Most days are spotted with small frustrations that continually test us. Often we may get frustrated when events don't happen to go the way we want. There are many roadblocks that we may run up against. At times it is hard being patient and understanding. Events need to be put into perspective. Often when we are injured or slighted we may tend to lash out. We should not get too upset. My mother-in-law frequently says, "Things do have a way of working out for the best."

> ## Keep your eyes on the stars and your feet on the ground.
> *Theodore Roosevelt*

Dream for the future. Look ahead. Make a goal for yourself. Act with caution. Balance dreams with some moderate common sense. If you have a dream, don't get stuck in the mud. Sometimes we may have to work overtime. Sometimes we may be excessive in pursuing our cause. We may be fueled by dreams of success. It does take a lot of sweat to be successful. Learn from the past: errors and success. Consult with teachers and advisors. Research your ideas. Make sure that you have the correct facts.

> ## Patience is a bitter plant, but it has sweet fruit.
> *German Proverb*

Patience often requires waiting. Today, I have no patience. I do not have time to wait. What I want, I want now! However after waiting over time, I may appreciate and value highly what I have waited for.

> ## Patience and diligence, like faith, remove mountains.
> *William Penn*

"Patience and diligence, like faith," require a lot of inner strength. Often serious problems cannot be solved overnight. Months and even years may need to pass until a solution occurs, but many great obstacles can be overcome.

> ## All commend patience, but none can endure to suffer.
> *Thomas Fuller, M.D.*

It is easy for you to tell me to be patient. How long must I wait? If I am in pain, how much more can I stand?

> ## Through anger, the truth looks simple.
> *Jane McCabe*

When I am angry I may distort what is happening. My thoughts may not be clear. I may have a tendency to reduce things to simple terms. It's not black and white. Often the truth has shades of gray. The actual truth is often more complicated.

Moderation – what to do:

1. Part of leading a life of moderation is a mental attitude to do actions in a moderate way. All the virtues can be done in moderation. Actions need to be thought out carefully rather than following extremes. We need to have balance in our lives. This begins in the morning with having breakfast and ends by making sure we have adequate rest at night.

2. We need to have a focus that being a happy person is a good goal to pursue. In a sense there are many wonderful things in the world for us to enjoy. However, we also need to balance that with the realization that our mortality may be around the corner. There was once a Sage who carried a piece of paper in one pocket on which was written, "All in the world was made for my use." In his other pocket was a note saying, "I am only food for the worms."

3. We need to maintain an attitude of not bearing grudges against other people. Small problems often become overblown. Pride often gets in the way of things. We expect things to be done for us which is a selfish attitude and needs to be moderated. Instead of telling my wife, "What have you done for me lately?" I remind myself, "What can I do for my wife to make her happy?" "What can I do" may involve cleaning dishes, yard work, child care, car pooling, and caring for elderly parents.

Moderation

4. Patience is a virtue that brings time into the equation of being moderate.
If I don't have the money to buy a new car, I need to have the patience to wait and save money every month. I can purchase a car later without going into too much debt.

5. Anger and pride are virtues that in extreme can be devastating and ruin a person's reputation and relationships. These virtues can at times be helpful. Being angry when an injustice occurs will help motivate us to make changes and correct the injustice. Having a trigger personality that explodes with minor problems only causes hurt feelings and may lead to potentially violent situations. For example, spouse beating either physically or with angry words is not acceptable behavior, and it is not a way to resolve marital disputes.

6. Use words of kindness when talking to a spouse. Don't use stinging words or sarcasm that will make the spouse cry. If we are angry, we will probably not be thinking clearly. Walk to another room in the house. Return in 15 or 30 minutes or when you feel calmed down and discuss the problem in a more rational way. It is amazing how a few minutes will put things in perspective.

Additional quotations on Moderation:

If you desire many things, many things will seem but a few.

Ben Franklin

Of cheerfulness, or a good temper –
    the more is spent, the more of it remains.

Emerson

He who is of a calm and happy nature will hardly feel
    the pressure of age, but to him who is of an opposite deposition,
    youth and age are equally a burden.

Plato

All music jars when the soul's out of tune.

Cervantes

Heat not a furnace for your foe so hot
    That it do singe yourself.

Shakespeare

To go beyond is as wrong as to fall short.

Confucius

Moderation

A middle course is always best.

Arab Proverb

The archer that shoots over,
     misses as much as he that falls short.

Montaigne

It is folly to punish your neighbor by fire
     when you live next door.

Publilius

Slow and steady wins the race.

Aesop

Moderation

Notes

Chapter 10
HEALTH

" Tolerate no uncleanness in body, cloths, or habitation," Franklin said. Cleanliness also relates to self-improvement. None of us are perfect. All of us have traits and bad habits that can be worked on and improved. Just as we set aside time to brush our teeth, we can also set aside time to reexamine ourselves and make ourselves better individuals.

Good health is often overlooked until illness occurs. There are things that we can actively do to keep ourselves in good health including eating in moderation and exercising on a regular basis. Preventive health care needs to be acted on by all of us. Consider the extreme costs of health care. By thinking preventive, we will contribute to our own future mental and financial security. Habits of smoking, alcohol and use of illegal drugs are hard to break. It is much easier not starting on a highly addictive habit than it is to break one. "Just saying no" seems superficial. Usually stress, unhappiness, and lack of opportunities serve as the source for addictive habits. It often takes a great deal of courage not to start bad habits, and it is even more difficult dealing with the sources.

> A man's habit clings
> And he will wear tomorrow what today he wears.
> *Edna St. Vincent Millay*

Our day is made of routines. It is hard to break from the routine and follow a new path. If I pick up habits, it is better to pick up good ones. A habit of daily walking or reading will give me much enjoyment. A habit of smoking will quietly destroy my life.

> Man like every other animal is by nature indolent.
> If nothing spurs him on, then he will hardly think,
> and will behave from habit like an automaton.
> *Albert Einstein*

Our living is repetitive and often out of habit. To change my ways, I will need a fire under me to make me change my direction.

> ## Health is not a condition of matter, but of Mind.
> Mary Baker *Eddy*

My attitude can determine if I am healthy. If I am inspired with dark thoughts, I may not value my life and may as well be thought of as near death. If I am in poor health, there is the opportunity for me to appreciate even something as minor as the ability to scratch my ear.

> ## The first wealth is health.
> *Emerson*

Wealth might refer to pleasure and enjoyment. Good health gives me pleasure. If good health leaves me, I become a poor man. It is difficult enjoying today when I sit in pain.

> ## A good garden may have some weeds.
> *Thomas Fuller, M.D.*

I often look at myself in a positive light and overlook my defects. My personality traits are sometimes weak and need improvement. I become angry at the wrong time. I am not appreciative of what people have done for me. Just like a garden has some weeds, we have weaknesses. In caring for a garden, weeds need to be removed at times and our weaknesses need improvement.

> ## No gains without pains.
> *Ben Franklin*

It is not easy following a regular program of improvement. The expression "no pain no gain" is often applied to sports. If I want to get better playing basketball, I am going to have to work and practice. If I want to make myself a better person, it will take time and work. It doesn't happen overnight, however, I can begin today.

Health – what to do:

1. **Eat in moderation and focus on a vegetarian based, high carbohydrate, low-fat diet.** Make regular aerobic exercise a priority. Walk 20 to 30 minutes four times per week. Other good aerobic activities include bicycle riding, jogging and swimming. Get adequate sleep of six to nine hours each night.

2. **Maintaining good health also entails having a positive attitude and a good feeling for oneself.** How is this done? Practice waking up each morning and saying, "What a great day it is and what a great person I am. I have many things to be grateful for. " Maintaining a positive attitude each day requires constant practice. If this is repeated each day, it may actually set the tone for the day and make the day a positive day.

3. **Count all the things that you are grateful for.** Visit a hospital or nursing home. We have a tendency to forget that we have hands and feet and eyes and hearing and lots of things that make our life a pleasure. This exercise of appreciating what we have makes what we don't have pale in comparison. Diversion of our mind away from what we are missing, and focusing on all that we have can be helpful. View the glass of water as half full, not half empty.

4. **We all have room for making some improvements and small changes in ourselves**. The attitude of wanting to be a better person needs to be learned. The best way to improve ourselves is to focus on helping other people. Involvement in community service or religious groups can be helpful.

5. **Smoking, alcohol and illegal drugs are things that we can choose to use or not use**. If we want to maintain a healthy body and a clear mind, however, these drugs need to be limited or not used at all. Smoking is clearly an addicting habit that has many serious long-term, adverse health effects. Alcohol in excess and frequent use can result in serious medical and social problems. Illegal psychoactive drugs can have subtle and major addictive tendencies and with frequent use can have multiple, irreversible toxic effects. These foolish actions detract from our health and our success.

6. In this modern era, sexual permissiveness is irresponsible behavior. HIV infection is in an epidemic throughout the world. There is no way for us to tell by looking at someone if they are HIV infected. We often get complacent and don't realize that any new sexual encounter could be a time bomb. Maintaining a monogamous relationship or abstinence are the only guarantees to avoid HIV infection.

7. As a physician I have seen many patients with poor eating habits, and lack of exercise. They all admit that it is good to eat properly and to exercise regularly. After discussing the benefits of making a change and having a discussion on how to start, the majority leave the office with good intentions but never change their habits. To make any change, no matter how small, is a difficult task which requires a major commitment by the patient. Many of us fall into the habit of saying, "Not today, but I will have time tomorrow." To begin, begin today. Perhaps you will never have time tomorrow.

Additional quotations on Health:

Health and appetite impart the sweetness to sugar, bread and meat.

Emerson

Growing is the reward of learning.   *Malcolm X*

There is no fruit which is not bitter before it is ripe.   *Publilius Syrus*

There is only one corner of the universe you can be certain of improving,
    and that's your own self.

Aldous Huxley

Take a two-mile walk every morning before breakfast.

Harry S Truman

There is a limit to the best of health:
disease is always a near neighbor.

Aeschylus

The shell must break before the bird can fly.

Alfred Lord Tennyson

The sum of the whole is this: walk and be happy;
    walk and be healthy.
The best way to lengthen our days is to walk
    steadily and with a purpose.
The wandering man knows of certain ancients,
    far gone in years, who have staved off
    infirmities and dissolution by earnest walking –
    hale fellows, close up on ninety, but brisk as boys.

Charles Dickens

Growth itself contains the germ of happiness.

Pearl S. Buck

Sickness is felt, but health not at all.

Thomas Fuller

If a child comes to school hungry,
the best school in the world won't help.

Arthur Ashe

Health

Notes

Chapter 11
CALMNESS

"Don't be disturbed by trifles or at unavoidable or common accidents," Franklin wrote. Avoid getting frustrated and angry. An angry person looses a great deal of his logic and sense. Raising one's voice in an angry tone will not improve the qualities of the arguments. Maintaining peace at home is a good goal. To have a peaceful home requires words and actions of kindness and honesty. Try to act with patience and compromise. This is no easy task. Little things that don't go the way we want them to go sometimes discourage us. At times we want to answer back with sharp words of anger. But usually within a few hours, the frustration passes and we regret having shown our anger. At times it is better to walk away from a disagreement rather than participate with angry words. Often we can return to a conflict later that day or the next day and be able to discuss a difficult problem with less heated words. Anger is a natural emotion that needs to be responsibly expressed without insulting the other person.

> When one door of happiness closes another opens;
> but often we look so long at the closed door that
> we do not see the one which has been opened for us.
>
> *Helen Keller*

There are an infinite number of activities that we can do which will give us pleasure. Most of them are transient. For a moment we are happy and then unhappiness settles in. We spend too much time focusing on what we have lost. Our mind is clouded. We don't appreciate all that we have.

> He is poor who does not feel content.
>
> *Japanese Proverb*

We do not appreciate what we have. We may not be able to see all that we have. We want more than what we have. We are not satisfied with what we live with. To feel contentment refers to achieving happiness by appreciating the little that we have.

> ## I've dealt with many crisis in my life, but few will ever happen.
> *Mark Twain*

We are continually confronted with frustrations and roadblocks. Many people try to discourage us. Often unsolvable, apparent problems will resolve with time and do not require action. We often imagine the worst case scenarios. Most of the time the apparent problem seems to go up into smoke. What a great moment when the bad doesn't occur.

> ## Discontent is the first step in the progress of a man or a nation.
> *Oscar Wilde*

Discontent presents itself as a problem. It is like a thorn in the side; it needs to be removed. Frustrations can often be turned around into opportunities. Look at bad fortune as an opportunity for progress. We are continually challenged with tough situations and tough people. View them as a challenge to overcome and learn from.

> It is neither wealth nor splendor,
> but tranquility and occupation,
> which give happiness.
>
> *Thomas Jefferson*

Most people strive for happiness. Poverty and sickness interfere with any sense of joy. Wealth is not a guarantee that a person will be content and happy. Splendor might refer to a life of fame but that is only transient. Tranquility refers to contentment with what you have. It is usually based on being grateful for all that you have even if you don't have much.

> It is easy to fly into a passion- anybody can do that-
> but to be angry with the right person to the right extent
> and at the right time and with the right object
> and in the right way-
> that is not easy, and it is not everyone who can do it.
>
> *Aristotle*

We often get angry over minor things. Trivial disagreements are often forgotten years later, but they result in quick words of hate and pain that stay with us and stick to our hearts and are not easily forgotten. Aristotle is suggesting that anger be done in a thoughtful, controlled way and as a tool to achieve a goal. Most of the time anger is viewed as a passionate expression of feelings without much thought. It takes wisdom and strength to express anger at the right time and in the right words.

Calmness-what to do:

1. **We often deal with many apparent crises that never really happen**. These events can throw us off balance. We need to recognize what things are really important. Keeping a list of what we value in front of us often helps remind us where our priorities are. When a crisis occurs I usually confide in my wife, friends or business advisors. They can serve as safety nets making the crisis easier to sail through.

2. **Being content with what we have requires some imagination**. Focus on what is valuable such as free time, visiting with family and friends, and education. How many successful businessmen are laying in their death beds, wishing that they had spent more time making business deals and regret the time they spent with their children?

3. **When bad events occur, they can be devastating**. However, in retrospect we often find that we have benefited from the bad experience more than we expected. Apparent bad luck may turn into good fortune. This attitude of accepting what happens and viewing it as a positive opportunity can contribute to much success. This attitude can be applied to small frustrating events or large world class problems.

4. **We need to take responsibility for our anger**. Uncontrollable anger or rage is unacceptable. Express anger when talking to another person without insulting and without attacking. Avoid blaming, accusing and fault finding. Express anger with assertive communication. Don't say, "You are lazy and no good." Instead say, "I am angry with you because...you didn't pick up your room when you said you would."

5. **Express your feelings** and let them know what behavior caused you to get upset and explain what they can do to correct their behavior in the future, "I am angry with you because... and I would like you to do..." "I sat for an hour waiting for you. You did not call me to warn me that you would be late. Next time call me as soon as you know you will be late."

6. **At times we need to look for compromise and a middle ground**, instead of expecting things to always go our way. Avoid absolutes in our demands. Avoid being rigid, inflexible and controlling. In implementing compromise we need to realize that we may not get or give all that we want. There may have to be some give and take until an equitable agreement is reached. Not all things are negotiable. It sometimes takes a great deal of thought and strategy in coming to a peaceful outcome.

7. **When encountering an angry person** sometimes saying to them, "You seem angry. Is there something I said that antagonized you?" may calm them down. If they persist, saying, "You seem angry, I would feel more comfortable discussing this more calmly. Let's meet later in 15 to 20 minutes," may turn off the steam.

8. **Chronic suppressed anger that is not expressed in some way may lead to illness and depression.** Healthy outlets for anger include physical exercise, gardening, hobbies, wood chopping, driving a car, getting out of the house, dancing, and playing music.

Additional quotations on Calmness:

When a man angers you, he conquers you.

Toni Morrison

You must be willing to suffer the anger of the opponent,
    and yet not return anger.
    No matter how emotional your opponents are,
    you must remain calm.

Martin Luther King, Jr.

My crown is called content;
    A crown it is that seldom kings enjoy.

Shakespeare

Calmness

Nothing will content him who is not content with a little.

Greek Proverb

Man is fond of counting his troubles, but he does not count his joys.
If he counted them up as he ought to, he would see that
every lot has enough happiness provided for it.

Dostoevsky

If you are bitter at heart, sugar in the mouth will not help you.

Yiddish Proverb

Up jumps the hare when you least expect it.

Hispanic Proverb

Patience serves as a protection against wrongs
as clothes do against cold,
for if you put on more cloths as the cold increases,
it will have no power to hurt you.
So in like manner you must grow in patience
when you meet with great wrongs,
and they will then be powerless to vex your mind.

Leonardo Da Vinci

It isn't the great big pleasures that count the most;
   it's making a great deal out of the little ones.

Jean Webster

The happy man is not he who seems thus to others,
   but who seems thus to himself.

Publilius Syrus

It is better to lose the saddle than the horse.

Italian Proverb

Compromise, if not the spice of life, is its solidity.

Phyllis McGinley

Keep cool:

anger is not an argument.

Daniel Webster

Notes

Chapter 12
FRIENDSHIP

Do not manipulate others. Ben Franklin said, "Protect your and other persons peace and reputation." A person needs to have respect for himself and for others. If we think poorly of ourselves, it becomes easy for others to think poorly of us. Try to view ourselves in a positive light. We all have good and bad qualities. Focus on your good qualities and strengthen them.

Show honor to others by speaking well of others. Avoid cutting down people. Show honor to your teachers and parents. Honor your teachers by being respectful to them. Honor your parents and friends by acting in a way that is positive not destructive.

Try not to embarrass a person. Try to view all people with respect. It is an error to use someone for selfish reasons. Many times people associate with other people for the wrong reasons. Look beyond the surface. Look for good qualities in people. Are they easy to be with? Are they kind? Are they sincere? Are they slow to anger? Or are they lazy? Do they complain? Are they always cutting people down? Choose your friends based on good qualities. Friendships based on good qualities tend to last.

> Be slow in choosing a friend, slower in changing.
> *Ben Franklin*

A friend might be someone to confide in, someone with whom to share difficult feelings. Look for someone who will have your best interests in heart. Friendships usually do not occur overnight. Trust develops between friends over time. I can depend on a friend based on their actions. My friend will not gossip about me. Friendships can be long lasting relationships. One good friend is precious. Put energy and time in maintaining the friendship. Don't give up a friendship so easily.

> Friendship with oneself is all-important, because without it
> one cannot be friends with anyone else in the world.
> *Eleanor Roosevelt*

Wake up each morning with a positive attitude and view yourself in a good way. Be grateful for all that you have. Friendship with oneself requires focusing on any good qualities that are present. If I have problems finding any good in myself and I dislike myself, I am focusing my images on bad and weakness. With such a negative mind set how can I possibly recognize your good qualities?

Friendship

> A true friend
> is the most precious of all possessions
> and the one we take the least thought about acquiring.
> *La Rochefoucauld*

During good times we will often have many friends, but only one or two will be with us during bad times. A true friend presents himself during difficult times. Usually he may not be recognized or even thought of as a friend. He becomes precious or valuable when we recognize and appreciate his actions of helping us. He is more valuable than diamonds. Look at how many "good guys" we know. How good are they? We need to be more careful about in whom we choose to invest our time and energy. Acquiring a friend requires some thought and planning. An important thing we can give our friend is our time.

> ## Do not use a hatchet to remove a fly from your friend's forehead.
> *Chinese proverb*

Use tact when you speak to your friend. If he is in trouble, use caution in giving him advice and help. Sometimes our advice is not wanted and it may cause more harm than good. A better strategy is just offer to listen.

> ## One learns people through the heart, not the eyes or the intellect.
> *Mark Twain*

To understand a person, we must have sensitivity. We use our understanding to empathize. As a friend we can share joy and heartbreak. With our eyes we may see only the superficial and be unable to penetrate to the truth. Our minds may not feel the pain. We will distance ourselves from our friend and make up rationalizations that will interfere with our closeness.

Friendship-what to do:

1. Sharing our time with another person is the best way to be friends. Invite them over for brunch over the weekend. Inquire about their interests and goals. Show an interest in them.

2. Friendship also means having respect for the other person. This applies to all people with whom you have contact including relatives, in-laws, spouses, and children. In essence we need to view each person with a good eye. We need to overlook their deficiencies and focus on their good qualities. Speaking positively with compliments and encouragement scores a lot of points compared to criticism and cutdowns.

3. We need to honor each person we encounter. It is wrong to treat people as if they are invisible or disposable. Manipulating people for selfish reasons is not appropriate. Friendships based on drugs, violence, money, status or sex are superficial and will not last. Take an interest in how your friends are doing. What have they recently accomplished? What problems are they encountering? How can you help out? Focus on helping friends rather than taking from them. Treat them the way you would want to be treated.

4. Friendship is often extended to children. Their innocence and trust can easily be taken advantage of. Sexual abuse of children by close adult friends and family members is a serious problem today which needs to be exposed and prevented. Children and adults need to be educated about abuse, keeping hands off certain private areas and maintaining appropriate behaviors. Children need to be taught at an early age not to keep secrets from their parents.

5. There is a fable that we were made with two eyes for a special reason. With our weaker, less critical eye we focus on our friends and see mainly their good qualities. With our stronger eye, we look inside ourselves and see our own weaknesses and try to improve them. Often I catch myself doing the opposite. It is often easy overlooking my own deficiencies. Fortunately my wife, who is also my friend, points out my weaknesses when I act too obnoxious.

Additional quotations on Friendship:

You cannot shake hands with a clenched fist.

Indira Gandhi

No man can be happy without a friend,
    nor be sure of his friend till he is unhappy.

Thomas Fuller

Good friends, good books, and a sleepy conscience:
    this is the ideal life.

Mark Twain

Your friend is the man who knows all about you
and still wants to be your friend.

Elbert Hubbard

Hold a true friend with both your hands.

Nigerian Proverb

Real friendship is shown during times of trouble;
prosperity is full of friends.

Euripides

Wishing to be friends is quick work,
but friendship is a slow-ripening fruit.

Aristotle

The love of our neighbor in all its fullness simply means
being able to say to him, "What are you going through?"
Simone Weil

In giving advice seek to help, not please your friend.
Solon

I have found the paradox that if I love until it hurts,
then there is no hurt, but only more love.
Mother Teresa

The only way to have a friend is to be one.   *Ralph Waldo Emerson*

But friendship is precious, not only in the shade,
        but in the sunshine of life:
and thanks to a benevolent arrangement of things,
        the greater part of life is sunshine.

                                        Thomas Jefferson

The only justification for ever looking down on somebody
        is to pick them up.

                                        Jesse L. Jackson

Treat all people as though they were related to you.

Navajo Proverb

He who sleeps with dogs will wake up with fleas.

Spanish Proverb

Friendship multiplies the good and minimizes misfortune

Baltasar Gracian

Notes

Chapter 13
MODESTY

When Franklin first developed his list of virtues he left out modesty. A friend pointed out to him that his speech was often argumentative and pompous. Franklin wrote, "I was not content with being right when discussing any point, but was overbearing and insolent." Franklin worked on this virtue by modifying the way he spoke. He focused on not contradicting others and respecting other opinions. He worked on diminishing his own assertive opinions. Opinions were presented in a more modest way. He avoided dogmatic expressions. There was less contradiction and abrasiveness.

Being modest does not refer to weakness and nonassertiveness. A modest person might let his actions speak rather than his words. Modesty needs to be balanced with a healthy sense of who we are. What are my strengths and weaknesses? If we feel comfortable with ourselves, we don't have to blow a horn to bring attention to ourselves. A modest mind-set does not need to wear fancy designer clothing or drive a status symbol automobile.

> **If** I am not for myself, who will be for me?
> And If I am only for myself, what am I?
> And if not now, when?
>
> *Hillel*

If I put little value in myself, others will not value me. This is a statement on a person's belief in himself and self-worth. If I do not have belief in myself, very few people will want to be with me. A person with poor self-worth faces a major struggle in work and relationships with other people. If I am self-centered and I don't have any real concern for others, I will be of little value to my community. A person needs to have a positive feeling about himself and yet balance it with concern for other people. And if not now, when? When refers to now. Today is when I can begin to accomplish the important things that need to be done.

> We should take care not to make
> the intellect our god;
> it has of course powerful muscles,
> but no personality.
>
> *Albert Einstein*

We can look at scientific study as having high value. What are we doing with all our knowledge? Where has it led us? Is this generation any more advanced and civilized than past less sophisticated ones? Scientific advances can be impressive and overwhelming. We can easily be enticed by its elegance and power. Often we are falsely led to believe that with scientific advances we can end poverty and war. "No personality" refers to a lack of human compassion. Einstein is putting the emphasis on personality. Character development is a great place to put our research and development dollars.

> Half of the harm that is done in this world
> is due to people who want to feel important.
>
> *T. S. Eliot*

Harm may refer to hurt feelings, cutdowns, belittling. We do this to others to make ourselves feel more important. But cutting down the other guy, it temporarily raises me up a few notches. Often this is done in an innocent way. It may even be justified by the common phrase, "but after all it is true!" Even if it is true, what purpose was obtained? Was it just innocent gossip?

Modesty

Modesty – what to do:

1. **Our speech reveals what we are**. If I pause and let someone say what he has to say without interrupting him, I am allowing him the opportunity to voice his opinion. If I interrupt him and cut down his opinion, I am acting in an arrogant way. Being less argumentative in speech and less openly critical of people's opinions is a modest action. Avoid phrases like "you are wrong," or "what an idiotic idea." Instead say, "I respect your opinion, however..." or "my opinion is...".

2. **Recognize that our gifts of thinking and creating can leave us at any moment**. When we are young we often feel so invincible. Human life is very fragile. How many individuals thought that they were on easy street with lots of money when a sudden reversal turned them upside down into a life of poverty or severe illness? Daily reminders of our vulnerability can change an arrogant attitude.

3. **Many successful people have the attitude that the money and property that they have is not their money and property**, but is kept by them in safekeeping to be used prudently for the benefit of those less fortunate in the world. The attitude of giving back something to society and feeling indebted to society are healthy attitudes to foster. Contributing time or money to charities, religious groups, and social organizations on a regular basis is one way of giving back to society.

Additional quotations on Modesty:

Humility is a strange thing, the minute you think you've got it, you've lost it.

E.D. Hulse

The bigger a man's head, the worse his headache.

Persian Proverb

The noisiest drum has nothing in it but air.

English Proverb

Whenever Nature leaves a hole in a person's mind,
    she generally plasters it over with a thick coat of self-conceit.

Longfellow

Every ass loves to hear himself bray.

Thomas Fuller

Pride is said to be the last vice the good man gets clear of.

Ben Franklin

The hurricane does not uproot grasses, which are pliant
and bow low before it on every side.
It is only the lofty trees that it attacks.

Panchatantra

The greatest deception men suffer is from their own opinions.

Leonardo Da Vinci

We are only falsehood, duplicity, contradiction;
we both conceal and disguise ourselves from ourselves.

Pascal

We are all worms,

but I do believe that I am a glow-worm.

Winston Churchill

Modesty

Notes

Addendum

In his autobiography, Franklin told a parable about a man who gave his axe to a blacksmith for sharpening and removal of speckling on the blade. As the axe was grinding, the man soon realized, "I think I like a speckled axe best." Franklin said, "A man without faults is a hateful creature. A good man should allow a few faults in himself, to keep his friends happy." We will always be speckled. Perhaps speckling adds some spice and variety. There will be many opportunities for us to slip and fall on our faces. Our failures and mistakes can be balanced with some optimism and humor. Fortunately there will be many more moments of happiness and success than failure.

There are major stresses that are fracturing contemporary American society. *What Counts* offers a framework of charting a sane course in an insane world. The virtues suggested by Ben Franklin are as timely now as they were in his day. The virtues serve as a guide on how we can behave. Attempting to improve ourselves seems to be a tall order. Begin one day at a time. Begin today, perhaps we will not have time tomorrow.

How did you use *What Counts*?

How did this book affect you?

Are there special quotations and ideas
that you would like to share with me?

Please share your thoughts by writing to me at…

Michael L. Loren, M.D.
17500 Medical Center Parkway
Independence, Mo 64057

or send a fax: 816-478-3413

To order additional copies of ***What Counts***
please send $7.95 in check or money order and $2 per book
to cover postage and handling.

Order through:

Overland Park Press
17500 Medical Center Parkway - Suite 6
Independence, MO 64057

(800) 241-9700

This book is available at special discount
when ordered in bulk quantities.